Nice girls don't wear CHA-CHA HEELS!

Leigh Rutledge

alyson books
los angeles | new york

© 1999 BY LEIGH RUTLEDGE. ALL RIGHTS RESERVED.

MANUFACTURED IN THE UNITED STATES OF AMERICA.
PRINTED ON ACID-FREE PAPER.
COVER DESIGN BY CHRISTOPHER HARRITY.

THIS TRADE PAPERBACK ORIGINAL IS PUBLISHED BY
ALYSON PUBLICATIONS,
P.O. BOX 4731, LOS ANGELES, CALIFORNIA 90078-4371
DISTRIBUTION IN THE UNITED KINGDOM BY
TURNAROUND PUBLISHER SERVICES LTD.,
UNIT 3 OLYMPIA TRADING ESTATE, COBURG ROAD, WOOD GREEN,
LONDON N22 6TZ ENGLAND.

FIRST EDITION: NOVEMBER 1999

99 00 01 02 03 a   10 9 8 7 6 5 4 3 2 1

ISBN 1-55583-440-X

COVER PHOTOGRAPH BY CHRISTOPHER HARRITY.

To my sister, Gayle,
who sneaked me into my first
R- and X-rated movies

For their assistance in helping me put this
volume together, I'd like to thank:
Bill Jump
Sam Staggs
Paul Hause
Randy Fizer
Scott Brassart
Richard Donley
Charlotte Simmons
Peter Urbanek

Contents

Introduction

Hollywood has always been at its worst when trying to be something it's not. Whether it's white actresses playing ethnic roles—who can forget Yvonne De Carlo writhing in misery as the overwrought Southern belle sold into slavery in *Band of Angels*?—or big-name stars giving soul-searching portrayals of angst-ridden artists (think of ultratan Merle Oberon and muscular Cornel Wilde portraying George Sand and tubercular Chopin in *A Song to Remember*), Hollywood has done its most achingly funny work when its reach exceeded its grasp.

Sex, for example, has always been on Hollywood's mind. Contrary to conservatives who build their political careers on a misbegotten yearning for the good old days, sex was an obsession even as the first silent features were being churned out at the beginning of the century. The Hays Production Code eventually gave the industry a thin veneer of high-mindedness and moral guardianship, but sex was still uppermost in Hollywood's mind—so while pretending to be sentinels of virtue and tradition, producers cranked out sexually ambivalent, sometimes sleazy melodramas full of double entendres, camp suggestiveness, and perfectly wardrobed actresses who indicated their hormone surges with convulsive, eye-rolling fits. The same was true with drugs. Small wonder that films like *Reefer Madness* achieved instant camp infamy even in their own time: Hollywood was sending out the obligatory message that drugs are *evil,* while much of the movie colony was notoriously high on booze, cocaine, marijuana, and heroin.

In the 1960s—as the topless bathing suit was being introduced to the world and X-rated movie houses began appearing closer and closer to the suburbs— Hollywood lacked the courage of its own convictions. Producers wanted films like *Harlow, The Carpetbaggers, Madame X,* and *Valley of the Dolls* to be titillating (the sexual revolution, after all, was nipping at everyone's heels) but not too titillating, nothing to offend housewives in Duluth, Minn., or Cincinnati. The result: All four movies, and countless others like them, became mother lodes of camp hilarity, nearly every line of dialogue an unbearable nugget of howling, often morbid suggestiveness.

Which leads us to one possible definition of camp: Camp is the real world made acceptable for people who have neither the wits nor the courage to understand it as it is. Hence, the drama of Moses is reduced to the panting, glossy superficiality of Cecil B. DeMille's *The Ten Commandments,* and Hollywood's notorious treadmill of casting couches becomes *Harlow*'s Carroll Baker as she whines, "Oh, Mama, all they want is my body!" But let's not get too serious. Trying to define camp is like killing a butterfly in hopes of quantifying and understanding its delicacy and appeal—no matter how pretty the result, it still smells of chloroform.

Nice Girls Don't Wear Cha-Cha Heels is a compendium of languid come-ons, snitty retorts, blasé metaphysics, jaded declarations of love, and histrionic expressions of lust from the movies. It's a world of listless debutantes, ruthless social climbers, long-suffering mothers, ambitious waitresses, sex-starved housewives, and women in bras staggering through hotel rooms while slugging down booze from a bottle. It's a book for all who have found themselves staring in stupefaction at *Valley of the Dolls* or convulsing with laughter through *Queen of Outer Space.* It is inevitable that some readers' favorites will not be here. This book represents my personal prejudices and tastes, prejudices accumulated from the time my mother dragged me to see a double feature of *The Oscar* and *Madame X* and I first began jotting down and collecting memorable camp lines.

—Leigh W. Rutledge, Key West, Fla.

If You Can't Say Anything Nice...

Columbia Pictures photo. Queen Bee © 1955, 1983 by Columbia Pictures Industries Inc.. All rights reserved. Used by permission.

Lucy Marlow, Joan Crawford, and Barry Sullivan in *Queen Bee*

"You're not a woman. You're a disease!"

—Mike Connors, *Where Love Has Gone* (1964)

"I thought you were a woman—but you're nothing but a career."

—Sterling Hayden to Bette Davis, *The Star* (1952)

"You're like some fancy kind of disease. I had it once—now I'm immune."

—John Ireland to Joan Crawford,
Queen Bee (1955)

"Floozy! Floozy! Floozy!"

—Carmen Miranda to Cobina Wright,
Week-End in Havana (1941)

"Usually, one must go to a bowling alley to meet a woman of your stature."

—John Gielgud, *Arthur* (1981)

"Look, if you think you're gonna get back in my panties, forget it. There's one asshole in there already."

—Kathleen Turner, *Crimes of Passion* (1984)

"Anne Schuyler's in the blue book. You're not even in the phone book."

—Edmund Breese, *Platinum Blonde* (1931)

"You, you're 42. There are many good minutes left for you."

—Milton Berle to Eleanor Parker, *The Oscar* (1960)

"You probably haven't had a good lay in years. Your legs have been together longer than the Lennon Sisters."

—Bette Midler, *Stella* (1990)

"You know something, Hank? You're 90% man and 10% rat!"

—Lana Turner, *Love Has Many Faces* (1965)

"THE STORK THAT BROUGHT YOU MUST HAVE BEEN A VULTURE."

—Ann Sheridan, *Torrid Zone* (1940)

"You have the touch of a love-starved cobra."

—Monty Woolley, *The Man Who Came to Dinner* (1941)

"As long as they've got sidewalks, you've got a job."

—Joan Blondell, *Footlight Parade* (1933)

"You're still a little shop girl from San Francisco. You should've stayed on the other side of the counter."

—Constance Bennett to Lana Turner, *Madame X* (1966)

"There are only two things I dislike about you—your face."

—Elizabeth Taylor to Kim Novak, *The Mirror Crack'd* (1980)

Sister number one (Bette Davis): "For some-one who just buried her husband this morn-ing, you don't seem very upset."
Sister number two (also Bette Davis): "Phony mourning makes me sick!"

—Bette Davis, *Dead Ringer* (1964)

"I detest cheap sentiment."

—Bette Davis, *All About Eve* (1950)

"Yes, I killed him. And I'm glad, I tell you. Glad, glad, *glad*!"

—Bette Davis, *The Letter* (1941)

"But ya are, Blanche, ya are in that chair."

—Bette Davis to Joan Crawford, *What Ever Happened to Baby Jane?* (1962)

"Mistress Throgmorton, is this your pet swine?"

—Bette Davis as Queen Elizabeth I, to Joan Collins, *The Virgin Queen* (1955)

"Oh, I wish Daddy could be here right now. You can never lose your talent, he used to tell me. You can lose everything else, but you can't lose your talent."

—Bette Davis, *What Ever Happened to Baby Jane?* (1962)

"TAKE YOUR 10% HANDS OFF ME!"

—Bette Davis to her agent,
The Star (1952)

"How about some pâté? Chock-full of vitamins!"

—Bette Davis, *Deception* (1946)

"June has some very *special* canapes for you!"

—Bette Davis, aggressive about hors d'oeuvres,
Now, Voyager (1942)

"George, I love you very much, but would you mind moving your chin just an inch to the right? Mammy spent an hour on these curls."

—Bette Davis, more concerned about her hair
than love, *Mr. Skeffington* (1944)

"What man would ever look at me and say 'I want you'? I'm fat. My mother doesn't approve of dieting. Look at my shoes. My mother approves of sensible shoes. Look at the books on my shelves. My mother approves of good, solid books. I am my mother's well-loved daughter. I am her companion. I am my mother's servant. My mother says—My mother, *my mother, MY MOTHER*!"

—Bette Davis, having a nervous breakdown,
Now, Voyager (1942)

11

"The only fun I get is feeding the goldfish, and they only eat once a day."

—Bette Davis, *Bordertown* (1935)

"I find one should never look for admirers while at the same time one is falling to bits."

—Bette Davis as the aging Fanny Skeffington,
Mr. Skeffington (1944)

"I'm so happy you're happy."

—Bette Davis to Celeste Holm,
All About Eve (1950)

PUT IT IN
YOUR MOUTH

"Two hot dogs, a pastrami for Francis, and a *very* large dill pickle for me."

—Jan Sterling, *The Female Animal* (1958)

"Anybody who could swallow two Sno Balls and a Ding Dong shouldn't have any trouble with pride!"

—Valerie Perrine to Steve Guttenberg, *Can't Stop the Music* (1980)

"She must have liked his brand of cream."

—Joan Blondell, gossiping about a friend who ran off with the milkman, *Will Success Spoil Rock Hunter?* (1957)

Little boy: "Cream?"
Little girl: "No, thank you. I take it black—like my men."

—David Hollander to Michelle Stacy,
Airplane! (1980)

"We were going to blonds next. Blonds were next on the menu. All that summer Sebastian was famished for blonds. Fed up with the dark ones. Famished for blonds."

—Elizabeth Taylor, *Suddenly, Last Summer* (1959)

"What do you have in your pocket?
A supply of wafers?"

—Alice Faye, *Week-End in Havana* (1941)

"Dorothy, didn't you notice? His pocket was bulging!"

—Marilyn Monroe, *Gentlemen Prefer Blondes* (1953)

"My balls are big enough to get your attention."

—Mickey Rourke, *Harley Davidson and the Marlboro Man* (1991)

"Honey, I was wondering, um——do you have two of anything else?"

—Chelsea Brown, *The Thing With Two Heads* (1972)

Fashion Victims

MGM Clip+Still photo. Stella Dallas © 1937 by Samuel Goldwyn Jr. Family Trust. All rights reserved. Used by permission.

Barbara Stanwyck in *Stella Dallas*

"I'm sure they're here. Oh, *where* is my head?"

—Norma Shearer as Marie Antoinette, looking for some
misplaced dresses, *Marie Antoinette* (1938)

**"Nice girls don't
wear cha-cha heels."**

—Roland Hertz to daughter Divine, *Female Trouble* (1974)

"Hysterectomy pants, I call 'em."

—Polly Bergen, *Cry-Baby* (1990)

"I've always been known to have stacks of style."

—Barbara Stanwyck, *Stella Dallas* (1937)

"I wouldn't be caught *dead* in a full skirt."

—Traci Lords, *Cry-Baby* (1990)

"You're going to see a smiling snatch
if you don't fix this G-string!"

—Angry chorus girl to wardrobe mistress,
Showgirls (1995)

"I remember every detail.
The Germans wore gray. You wore blue."

—Humphrey Bogart to Ingrid Bergman, *Casablanca* (1942)

"AH, THE SHAPE OF THINGS TO COME!"

—Advertising line used with a picture of Yvette Mimieux in a skimpy dress, for *The Time Machine* (1960)

"I KNOW EXACTLY HOW YOU FEEL, MY DEAR. THE MORNING AFTER ALWAYS DOES LOOK GRIM IF YOU HAPPEN TO BE WEARING LAST NIGHT'S DRESS."

—Ina Claire to Greta Garbo, *Ninotchka* (1939)

*"What are you supposed
to be—a birthday cake?
Too bad everyone's had a piece."*

—Elizabeth Taylor, dishing Kim Novak's outfit,
The Mirror Crack'd (1980)

"Remember, my people, there is
no shame in being poor,
only dressing poorly."

—George Hamilton, *Zorro, the Gay Blade* (1981)

22

"Would you be surprised to know that this rough, tough individual was wearing pink satin undies under his rough exterior clothing? He is. This person is a transvestite, a man who is more comfortable wearing girls' clothes. One might say: There but for the grace of God go I."

—Narrator, *Glen or Glenda* (1953)

"Honey, I'm more man than you'll ever be—and more woman than you'll ever get."

—Antonio Fargas, to gay bashers,
Car Wash (1976)

"Bring them out that we may kno-o-ow them."

—Uncredited drag queen with intense eye makeup in the Sodom and Gomorrah segment, *The Bible* (1966)

"There's something that gives me a queer feeling every time I look at you."

—Cary Grant to Katharine Hepburn, *Sylvia Scarlett* (1935)

"That was Somerset Maugham on the telephone. He always gives me the queerest feeling."

—Gene Tierney, *The Razor's Edge* (1946)

"OUT WHERE THEY SAY, 'LET US BE GAY'—I'M GOING HOLLYWOOD!"

—Bing Crosby, *Going Hollywood* (1933)

"For two bachelors, you seem to know a great deal about what women wear."

—Maureen O'Sullivan, *Tarzan and His Mate* (1934)

"Oh, honey, I'd be so happy if you turned nelly. Queers are just better. I'd be so proud if you was a fag and had a nice beautician boyfriend. I'd never have to worry. I worry you'll work in an office, have children, celebrate wedding anniversaries. The world of a heterosexual is a sick and boring life!"

—Edith Massey to her nephew,
Female Trouble (1974)

"*Ted Casablanca is not a fag!
And I'm the dame to prove it!* "

—Patty Duke, *Valley of the Dolls* (1967)

"**Life's a queer little man, kiddie.**"

—Wendell Corey, *The Big Knife* (1955)

"Don't you know that a man being rich is like a girl being pretty? You might not marry a girl because she's pretty, but——my goodness——doesn't it help?"

—Marilyn Monroe, *Gentlemen Prefer Blondes* (1953)

"I wasn't always rich. No, there was a time I didn't know where my next husband was coming from."

—Mae West, *She Done Him Wrong* (1933)

"I can't marry you until I get my hearing back. I just can't make you go through life watching me stare at other people's lips."

—Loretta Young as a deaf woman,
And Now Tomorrow (1944)

"I'M NOT GOOD ENOUGH TO MARRY. I'M NOT GOOD ENOUGH TO KISS."

—Jennifer Jones, *Duel in the Sun* (1946)

"YOUR GARDENER?"

—Agnes Moorehead, aghast at Jane Wyman's announcement that she intends to marry the man who trims her trees, Rock Hudson, *All That Heaven Allows* (1955)

"Tarzan, I've practically *begged* you to fix that shower, and here you just sit…"

—Brenda Joyce, nagging Johnny Weismuller about repairs to the jungle treehouse, *Tarzan and the Leopard Woman* (1946)

"I'm sorry I spoiled your day by asking you to be my wife."

—Laurence Harvey to Capucine, *Walk on the Wild Side* (1962)

"Let's not linger over it."

—Bette Davis, breezily breaking off her engagement
to fiancé John Loder, *Now, Voyager* (1942)

"You'll make a lovely bride. And I'm sure
you'll give my son a big *bonefest*
of a honeymoon."

—Joan Plowright to Ellen DeGeneres, *Mr. Wrong* (1996)

"Hello, everybody. This is Mrs. Norman Maine."

—An emotionally overwrought Judy Garland at
the final fade-out of *A Star Is Born* (1954)

"You've never done anything to make your mother proud. Or to make yourself proud either. Why, I should think you'd be ashamed to be born and live all your life as Charlotte Vale—*Miss* Charlotte Vale."

—Gladys Cooper to daughter Bette Davis,
Now, Voyager (1942)

"ALL YOU HAVE TO DO IS TURN THE DIAL, AND YOU HAVE ALL THE COMPANY YOU WANT. COMEDY, DRAMA—LIFE'S PARADE AT YOUR FINGERTIPS!"

—Perky TV salesman to lonely widow
Jane Wyman, *All That Heaven Allows* (1955)

Food and Drink

"How many times must I tell you? Queens consume nectars and ambrosia, not hot dogs. "

—Victor Buono as King Tut, to his
uncouth consort, *Batman* (1966)

"Honey, you're a mess. You better stop eating those chocolates."

—Marlene Dietrich to Orson Welles,
Touch of Evil (1958)

"BEULAH, PEEL ME A GRAPE."

—Mae West, *I'm No Angel* (1933)

"And Caleb, the fatted calf, bring
the fatted calf, for this night we
shall eat and make merry!"

—Walter Hampden, *The Prodigal* (1955)

"Fetch me a mai-tai, Ping-Pong."

—Angela Lansbury to an Asian servant,
Blue Hawaii (1961)

"WHY DON'T YOU SLIP OUT OF THOSE
WET CLOTHES AND INTO A DRY MARTINI?"

—Robert Benchley to Ginger Rogers,
The Major and the Minor (1942)

"Keep drinking, honey. I like you better drunk than sober."

—Burgess Meredith to Lana Turner, *Madame X* (1966)

"She's not going to die. She just thinks she is. She's drunk!"

—Hedy Lamarr, *The Female Animal* (1958)

"HE WAS TRYING TO SEDUCE ME—WITH DOMESTIC CHAMPAGNE!"

—Susan Hayward, *Back Street* (1961)

"I was brought up on goat's milk, had a ration of vodka in the army, and now—champagne!"

—Greta Garbo, *Ninotchka* (1939)

"God opens the sea with a blast of his nostrils!"

—Uncredited older man, *The Ten Commandments* (1956)

"OH, MOSES, MOSES. YOU STUBBORN, SPLENDID, ADORABLE FOOL!"

—Anne Baxter, *The Ten Commandments* (1956)

"Delilah, what a dimpled dragon you can be."

—George Sanders to Hedy Lamarr,
Samson and Delilah (1949)

"I never thought of Jesus being so *tall*!"

—Uncredited girl stroking Christ's crucifixion robe,
Demetrius and the Gladiators (1954)

"Your first crucifixion, isn't it?"

—Roman centurion Jeff Morrow making precrucifixion small
talk with Richard Burton, *The Robe* (1953)

"Christians… Are they the ones who worship
some dead carpenter?"

—Uncredited Roman centurion,
Quo Vadis (1951)

"The golden Samara herself and the high sacrifice besides *and* the fertility rite. Master, there is nothing like it on the square face of the earth!"

—Joseph Wiseman, *The Prodigal* (1955)

"YOU PHILISTINE GUTTER RAT!"

—Victor Mature to Hedy Lamarr, *Samson and Delilah* (1949)

"Joshua will always be grateful to you, my little mud flower."

—Edward G. Robinson, *The Ten Commandments* (1956)

"You are a true Sodomite, Lot."

—The queen of Sodom, Anouk Aimee, congratulating
Stewart Granger on his assimilation into the city,
Sodom and Gomorrah (1963)

HISTORY 101

"Queens! Queens! Strip 'em as naked as any other woman and they're no longer queens!"

—Richard Burton as Mark Antony, *Cleopatra* (1963)

"WHAT'S THE MATTER, MATA?"

—Ramon Novarro to Greta Garbo,
Mata Hari (1932)

"This Tartar woman is for me! My blood says 'Take her!'"

—John Wayne as Genghis Khan,
The Conqueror (1956)

"Don't shout! I'm not deaf!"

—Albert Bassermann as Beethoven,
New Wine (1941)

"YOU DARE TO DICKER WITH YOUR PONTIFF!"

—Rex Harrison as Pope Julius II to Charlton Heston as Michelangelo,
The Agony and the Ecstasy (1965)

"No better day for marrying, the breeding of cattle, or the offering up of blood sacrifices."

—Louis Calhern as the high priest, checking
the auguries, *The Prodigal* (1955)

"My, that's fast! It sounds like a bee or something..."

—Yvonne De Carlo to Jean-Pierre Aumont as composer Nikolai Rimsky-Korsakov, while he performs a little piece on the piano, later to be called "The Flight of the Bumble Bee," *Song of Scheherazade* (1947)

"HENRI, WE HEARD YOU WERE DYING AND WE CAME TO SAY GOODBYE!"

—Zsa Zsa Gabor to Jose Ferrer as Toulouse-Lautrec, *Moulin Rouge* (1952)

"She died of life."

—Red Buttons, at the deathbed of Carroll Baker, *Harlow* (1965)

When Strangers Meet

"Guests—what good are they? Do they come because they like you? No. They come to throw sandwiches into the pool and make person-to-person calls to the moon!"

—Lana Turner, *Love Has Many Faces* (1965)

"Strange faces frighten me. Even handsome ones."

—Maria Montez, *Cobra Woman* (1944)

"That's a lot of man you're carrying in those boots, stranger."

—John Carradine to Sterling Hayden, *Johnny Guitar* (1954)

"Your food tempts me not. Do not touch me. You smell of fish."

—Foreign princess Joyce Taylor to her rescuer, Anthony Hall,
Atlantis: The Lost Continent (1960)

"I always so terribly wanted to meet a young man. And now, three of them at once! You're lovely, doctor. Of course, the two end ones are unbelievable!"

—Anne Francis, sizing up the crew of the recently
arrived space cruiser C-57D,
Forbidden Planet (1956)

"I have always depended on the kindness of strangers."

—Vivien Leigh, *A Streetcar Named Desire* (1951)

"I speak several languages, I play the piano, I can converse intelligently, and I have good teeth. Would you like to examine them?"

—Mail-order bride Eleanor Parker to Charlton Heston,
The Naked Jungle (1954)

"There I was, with a perfectly strange plumber—and no polish on my toenails!"

—Marilyn Monroe, *The Seven Year Itch* (1955)

"Well, what do you know—marines! Seven thousand miles from the States, and I'm right at home! Got me a couple of hours to kill between boats. What's to do around here, fellas? Got any attractions? You know, grass skirts, hula hulas, all that island stuff?"

—Rita Hayworth, *Miss Sadie Thompson* (1953)

"A girl gets just what she asks for. And all I'm asking for is company on a rainy night."

—Rita Hayworth, *Miss Sadie Thompson* (1953)

"YOUR BEAUTY AND CHARMS ARE BEYOND COMPARE. BUT CAN YOU WEAVE A SADDLE BLANKET FROM THE WOOL OF A NUBIAN GOAT? OR PLAIT A HORSEHAIR ROPE?"

—Jeff Chandler to visitor Maureen O'Hara, *Flame of Araby* (1951)

Love

"I just can't throw myself at him! He'd only step over me on his way to the piano."

—Joanne Dru, fretting over her infatuation
with Liberace, *Sincerely Yours* (1955)

"The Venus flytrap—a devouring organism, aptly named for the goddess of love."

—Katharine Hepburn, *Suddenly, Last Summer* (1959)

"I NEVER KNEW IT TO FAIL. SOME BIG, HARD-BOILED EGG GETS A LOOK AT A PRETTY FACE AND—BANG!—HE CRACKS UP AND GOES SAPPY!"

—Robert Armstrong, on King Kong's infatuation with Fay Wray, *King Kong* (1933)

"L'amour! L'amour! Toujours l'amour!"

—Mary Boland, *The Women* (1939)

"'I love you' is such an inadequate way of saying I love you."

—Joan Crawford, *Possessed* (1947)

"ALL YOU LOVE IS MY DICK."

—Vincent D'Onofrio to Lili Taylor, *Mystic Pizza* (1988)

"*No tongue! I'm wearing lipstick!*"

—Diane Ladd, *Wild at Heart* (1990)

"The first time I saw you, I hated your guts. I think I even hated you before I met you. I hated you on TV. I hated you in Vietnam. You know what's destroying this country? It's not booze. It's not drugs. It's TV. It's media. It's people like you. It's vampires. I hate the way you make your living sticking microphones in people's faces. You lie every night at 6 o'clock. I hate the way you kill real feelings. I hate everything you stand for. Most of all, I hate rich kids, and I hate this place. So why do I want to fuck you so bad?"

—Mickey Rourke, *Year of the Dragon* (1985)

"You can fuck me when you love me."

—Elizabeth Berkley to Glenn Plummer, *Showgirls* (1995)

"For two years I've been lost, like walking in my sleep. Suddenly I wake up—that's you. I don't know what I've been doing all that time waiting for you without knowing it. Do you know what you are to me? Paris. That's you. Paris. With you, I escape. Follow me? The whole town, a spring morning in Paris. You're lovely. You're marvelous. And do you know what you remind me of? The subway. You're all silk, and you jingle when you walk. And with all that chi-chi, you make me think of the subway. And potato chips."

—Charles Boyer to Hedy Lamarr, *Algiers* (1938)

"I'M YOUR NUMBER 1 FAN."

—Kathy Bates to James Caan, *Misery* (1990)

"You're so…so good for what ails me."

—Lana Turner to John Gavin, *Imitation of Life* (1959)

"My diary is simply full of him!"

—Jeanne Crain, in love with her French teacher,
Glenn Langan, *Margie* (1946)

"All I know about you is that you stole my car—and I'm insane about you!"

—Gary Cooper to Marlene Dietrich,
Desire (1936)

"I'm the beggar, Moses. Begging you to take me in your arms! Kiss me! Just kiss me!"

—Anne Baxter to Charlton Heston,
The Ten Commandments (1956)

"I'd love to kiss ya, but I jes washed mah hair."

—Bette Davis, *Cabin in the Cotton* (1932)

A Sick Woman

"Mother, my mother—what is the phrase?— she isn't quite herself today."

—Anthony Perkins, *Psycho* (1960)

"It's the brain. The only brain she ever had was subnormal, in some ways subhuman."

—Otto Kruger, *Jungle Captive* (1945)

"She suffers from something called dementia precox, which is to say she's mad as a hatter, poor child."

—Katharine Hepburn, *Suddenly, Last Summer* (1959)

"SHE'S A SICK WOMAN."

—Marjorie Bennett to Joan Crawford, in regard to Bette Davis, *What Ever Happened to Baby Jane?* (1962)

"You must be very gentle with her. She has an advanced Electra complex."

—Raymond Greenleaf, discussing Cornell Borchers, *Never Say Goodbye* (1956)

"Cut off her nipples with gardenin' shears! Ya call that *normal?*"

—Elizabeth Taylor, discussing Julie Harris,
Reflections in a Golden Eye (1967)

"I always look well when I'm near death."

—Greta Garbo, *Camille* (1936)

MGM Clip+Still photo. Bull Durham © 1988 by Orion Pictures Corp. All rights reserved. Used by permission.

Tim Robbins and Susan Sarandon in *Bull Durham*

"Come on, boys, and carry my bananas!"

—Mamie Van Doren, *Girls Town* (1959)

"IF I'D BEEN A RANCH, THEY WOULD'VE NAMED ME THE BAR NOTHING."

—Rita Hayworth, *Gilda* (1946)

"Later, when all my guests are gone, I will be here, by my lotus pool."

—Egyptian femme fatale Bella Darvi,
The Egyptian (1954)

"When it's hot like this you know what I do? I keep my undies in the icebox."
—Marilyn Monroe, *The Seven Year Itch* (1955)

"Oh, I'm so tired of just being pretty."
—Kim Novak, *Picnic* (1955)

"Oh, I'm bored. And I've only just gotten up."
—Capucine, *Walk on the Wild Side* (1962)

"Oh, God. Not another fucking beautiful day."

—Sarah Miles, *White Mischief* (1988)

"It wasn't the first time I went to bed with a guy and woke up with a note."

—Susan Sarandon, *Bull Durham* (1988)

"ALL MY LIFE I'VE BEEN FED IDEALS INSTEAD OF *FUN!*"

—Diane McBain, *Parrish* (1961)

"SHE WAS A 12 O'CLOCK GIRL IN A 9 O'CLOCK TOWN!"

—Advertising tagline used to describe Bette Davis's
character, *Beyond the Forest* (1949)

"I've had more fun in the back of a '39 Ford than I could ever have in the vault of the Chase National Bank!"

—Elizabeth Taylor, *Butterfield 8* (1960)

"Ann, honey, let's face it—all I know how to do is take off my clothes."

—Sharon Tate, *Valley of the Dolls* (1967)

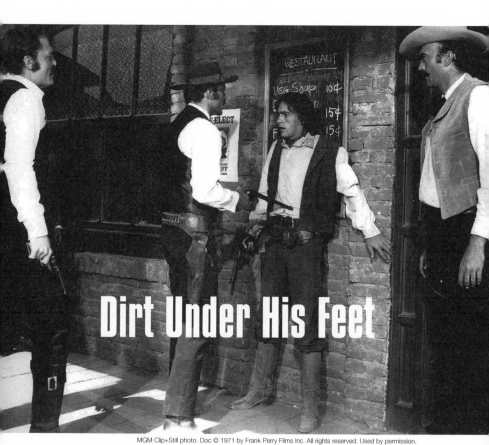

Dirt Under His Feet

MGM Clip+Still photo. Doc © 1971 by Frank Perry Films Inc. All rights reserved. Used by permission.

The men from *Doc*

"I treated her like a pair of gloves.
When I was cold I called her up."

—Cornel Wilde, *The Big Combo* (1955)

"Mistreat me, make love to me, anything. Only get it over with. Then throw me out."

—Carroll Baker, *The Carpetbaggers* (1964)

"You kinda get turned on by a guy who treats you nice, like the schlep you were out with tonight. But a guy who wipes his feet on you—that you *dig*!"

—Stephen Boyd, *The Oscar* (1966)

72

"He's no good, but he's what I want."

—Judith Anderson, *Laura* (1944)

"You can't just toss me around like a football!"

—Glynis Johns, *The Chapman Report* (1962)

"Look at me when you talk to me! I'm not some sort of garbage pail you can slam a lid on and walk away from! Let me tell you about hell, about being a silly woman who needs to feel she belongs to someone—even someone as empty as you are, Frankie!"

—Eleanor Parker, *The Oscar* (1966)

"You like to get hurt. Always picking the wrong guy. It's a sickness with a lot of women. Always looking for a new way to get hurt by a new man."

—Richard Conte to Susan Hayward,
House of Strangers (1949)

"A woman's no good to a man unless she's a little bit afraid of him."

—Jeff Chandler, *Female on the Beach* (1955)

"When you're slapped you'll take it and like it!"

—Humphrey Bogart, *The Maltese Falcon* (1941)

Mother

"No wire hangers! What's wire hangers doing in this closet when I told you no wire hangers ever?"

—Faye Dunaway, *Mommie Dearest* (1981)

"SING OUT, LOUISE! SING OUT!"

—Rosalind Russell, *Gypsy* (1962)

"What if I do want them to amount to something? I'll do anything for those kids! Do you understand? *Anything*!"

—Joan Crawford, *Mildred Pierce* (1945)

"Don't mind grandma. She's kinda nuts about sin and stuff like that."

—Connie Stevens, *Parrish* (1961)

"Could we try to remember that we're hardly commercial travelers? Bad enough to have to associate with these tourists!"

—Gladys Cooper to long-suffering daughter Bette Davis, *Now, Voyager* (1942)

"Mother's tired. Come stick pins tomorrow morning. I'll be more responsive."

—Katharine Hepburn, *The Lion in Winter* (1968)

"My mother! What did you ever do to earn that title except pay a couple of bills?"

—Jane Powell to Hedy Lamarr, *The Female Animal* (1958)

"MY MOTHER. A WAITRESS!"

—Ann Blyth, *Mildred Pierce* (1945)

"A woman who cannot bear children is like a river that is dry."

—Elizabeth Taylor, *Cleopatra* (1963)

"I'm not mad at you, Helga.
I'm mad at the dirt."

—Faye Dunaway, *Mommie Dearest* (1981)

"She might have fooled me, but she didn't fool my mother."

—Anthony Perkins, *Psycho* (1960)

"How do you tell your baby she was born to be hurt?"

—Juanita Moore, *Imitation of Life* (1959)

"We were a famous couple. People didn't speak of Sebastian and his mother. Or Mrs. Venable and her son. No, they said 'Sebastian and Violet. Violet and Sebastian are staying at the Lido. They're at the Ritz in Madrid.' And every appearance, every time we appeared, attention was centered on us. Everyone else was eclipsed."

—Katharine Hepburn, *Suddenly, Last Summer* (1959)

An Eye for Beauty

"PEARL, YOU'RE CURVED IN THE FLESH OF TEMPTATION. RESISTANCE IS GOING TO BE A DARN SIGHT HARDER FOR YOU THAN FOR FEMALES PROTECTED BY THE SHAPE OF SOWS."

—Walter Huston to Jennifer Jones,
Duel in the Sun (1946)

"I'm not bad. I'm just drawn that way."

—Voice of Kathleen Turner as Jessica Rabbit,
Who Framed Roger Rabbit (1988)

"For a cheese maker, he has bold eyes."

—Egyptian princess Gene Tierney, appraising
Victor Mature, *The Egyptian* (1954)

"Did you not notice how superb were the haunches of the Grecian woman?"

—Lana Turner, *The Prodigal* (1955)

"You have a shrewd eye, your pulchritude."

—Slave trader Peter Ustinov to shopper Joanna Barnes,
Spartacus (1960)

"Your hair is like a field of daisies. I should like to run barefoot through your hair."

—Franchot Tone to Jean Harlow,
Bombshell (1933)

"Your lips are made for kissing. They're like the inner petals of a rose."

—Rossano Brazzi, *Rome Adventure* (1962)

"He got a real pretty mouth, ain't he?"

—Mountainman, admiring Jon Voight's lips,
Deliverance (1973)

"She looks better than a 10-inch dick."

—Lin Tucci, *Showgirls* (1995)

"PEOPLE WHO ARE VERY BEAUTIFUL MAKE THEIR OWN LAWS."

—Vivien Leigh, *The Roman Spring of Mrs. Stone* (1961)

Women

"Oh, thou, my God, save thy servant that trusteth in thee. Save him from this bigmouthed cooz with the motor-driven ass."

—Anthony Perkins, *Crimes of Passion* (1984)

"You're just like every woman! You're dirty, you lie, you cheat! You oughta be wiped off the face of the earth, every one of you! *Every one of you!*"

—Edward Andrews to Esther Williams, *The Unguarded Moment* (1956)

"There are more women in the world than anything else—except insects."

—Glenn Ford to Rita Hayworth, *Gilda* (1946)

"I love her! I hate her! I adore her!"

—Errol Flynn as the Earl of Essex, mad about Bette Davis as Queen Elizabeth I, *The Private Lives of Elizabeth and Essex* (1939)

"I make rough seas. I set the jungle on fire. I'm a bad influence."

—Marlene Dietrich, *Seven Sinners* (1940)

"THEY SAY A MOONLIT DECK IS A WOMAN'S BUSINESS OFFICE."

—Barbara Stanwyck, *The Lady Eve* (1941)

AFD photo. Can't Stop the Music © 1980 by Associated Film Distribution. All rights reserved. Used by permission.

Steve Guttenberg, Valerie Perrine, and Bruce Jenner in *Can't Stop the Music*

"You're not a man. You're a golf bag!"

—Margaret Lindsay to James Whitmore, *The Restless Years* (1958)

**"You're not too smart, are you?
I like that in a man."**

—Kathleen Turner, *Body Heat* (1981)

*"I like big muscles and red corpuscles.
I like a beautiful hunk of man."*

—Sung by Jane Russell,
Gentlemen Prefer Blondes (1953)

DAUGHTER: "HE'S BOSSY AND RUDE AND STUPID."
FATHER: "AND YOU LOVE HIM?"
DAUGHTER: "YES, DARN IT."

—Francis Dee and Edward Ellis,
Wheel of Fortune (1941)

"God is good. He sent me a big, strong man."

—Lilia Skala, *Lilies of the Field* (1963)

"Fruit of the Loom is doing a big ad campaign. Something tells me you could really fit into a pair of Jockey shorts."

—Tammy Grimes to Bruce Jenner,
Can't Stop the Music (1980)

"Why, George, you have a real hate-on!"

—Shelley Winters to Peter Falk, *The Balcony* (1963)

"YOU JUST CAN'T MAKE UP YOUR MIND, CAN YOU? REPENT ONE MINUTE, SLOBBER THE NEXT."

—Ann Sothern to Jeffy Corey,
Lady in a Cage (1964)

"It took more than one man to change my name to Shanghai Lily."

—Marlene Dietrich, *Shanghai Express* (1932)

Dating

"Peggy Sue, do you know what a penis is? Please, Peggy Sue—stay away from it!"

—Barbara Harris to daughter Kathleen Turner,
Peggy Sue Got Married (1986)

"That's why I worry—thinking of you coming up against those young, tight sweaters."

—Mamie Van Doren to teenage nephew Russ Tamblyn,
High School Confidential (1958)

"A low neckline does more for a girl's future than the entire Britannica encyclopedia!"

—Terry Moore, *Peyton Place* (1957)

"I can see your dirty pillows!"

—Piper Laurie, horrified that daughter Sissy Spacek's
prom dress shows cleavage, *Carrie* (1976)

**"My brother wouldn't touch your titties with a 10-foot pole.
He likes his women bad, Leonora, not cheap."**

—Ricki Lake, *Cry-Baby* (1990)

"He's dating the devil in a maiden's form."

—Lane Chandler, *Take Me to Town* (1953)

"And now I will show you the greatest secret of all—how to make your eyes look deep and dark and mysterious."

—Lana Turner, counseling a young protégé on the fine points of being irresistible to men, *The Prodigal* (1955)

"When one is young, one should use lots of mascara. And when one is older, one should use *much* more."

—Sybil Thorndike, *The Prince and the Showgirl* (1957)

"You can't let him think your kisses come cheap!"

—Constance Ford to daughter Sandra Dee, *A Summer Place* (1959)

TRAMP!

MGM Clip+Still photo. By Love Possessed © 1961 by United Artists Pictures Inc. All rights reserved. Used by permission.

George Hamilton, Barbara Bel Geddes, and Efram Zimbalist Jr. in *By Love Possessed*

"When I'm down on my knees,
I ain't praying!"

—Faye Dunaway, *Doc* (1971)

"Face it, Mama. I was the slut of all time!"

—Elizabeth Taylor, *Butterfield 8* (1960)

**"Go ahead and say it. I'm a dumb,
cheap tramp. Go ahead and say it!"**

—Connie Stevens, *Parrish* (1961)

**"She's been around more in her 20 years than
the moon in its millions."**

—Thomas Mitchell, *By Love Possessed* (1961)

"You dance lewdly for the boys at lunch period?"

—Divine, horrified at how her daughter earns
pocket money, *Polyester* (1981)

"You better run, you little tramp!
How dare you contaminate my pool!"

—Patty Duke, to her husband's girlfriend,
Valley of the Dolls (1967)

"Man, she looked as if she'd just been thrown off the
crummiest freight train in the world."

—Tom Neal, *Detour* (1945)

"I've been passed from hand to hand.
Armies have marched over me."

—Rita Hayworth, *Fire Down Below* (1957)

"They don't have to see her. They can *smell* her."

—Orson Welles, talking about his daughter, Joanne Woodward,
The Long Hot Summer (1958)

"We may as well face it. I've gone to the dogs."

—Natalie Wood, *Marjorie Morningstar* (1958)

"I'm trash, I tell you. Trash!"

—Jennifer Jones, *Duel in the Sun* (1946)

"What hole did you crawl *out* of?"

—Mel Torme to Mamie Van Doren,
Girls Town (1959)

Show Business

AFD photo. The Mirror Crack'd © 1980 by Associated Film Distribution. All rights reserved. Used by permission.

Elizabeth Taylor and Rock Hudson in *The Mirror Crack'd*

"I AM BIG! IT'S THE PICTURES THAT GOT SMALL!"

—Gloria Swanson, *Sunset Boulevard* (1950)

"I could eat a can of Kodak and puke a better movie!"

—Kim Novak, *The Mirror Crack'd* (1980)

"You don't belong to any man now. You belong to Broadway!"

—Adolph Menjou, *Morning Glory* (1933)

"You're going out a youngster, but you've got to come back a star!"

—Warren Baxter, *42nd Street* (1933)

"YOU'RE THE *TIMES* IN TIMES SQUARE! YOU'RE THE *BROAD* IN BROADWAY!"

—Agent to Joan Crawford, *Torch Song* (1953)

"My dear boy, one does need a little talent in this business—but not necessarily for acting."

—Jan Sterling, *The Female Animal* (1958)

"It's your music that's bringing all these talented boys together. They ought to get down on their knees!"

—June Havoc to Steve Guttenberg, in reference to the Village People, *Can't Stop the Music* (1980)

Trashy Leftovers

MGM Clip+Still photo. Carrie © 1976 by United Artists Corp. All rights reserved. Used by permission.

Sissy Spacek and Piper Laurie in *Carrie*

"I wouldn't suck your lousy dick if I was suffocating and there was oxygen in your balls!"

—Divine, *Female Trouble* (1977)

"I shoulda killed myself the first time he put it in me!"

—Piper Laurie, *Carrie* (1976)

"Why don't you run outside and jerk yourself a soda?"

—Annette Bening to Warren Beatty,
Bugsy (1991)

"Why don't you go bingle your bongle!"

—Mamie Van Doren to a lesbian in
reform school, *Girls Town* (1959)

"I'm so tired of being good."

—Amy Locane, *Cry-Baby* (1990)

"Marcia, Marcia, Marcia!"

—Jennifer Elise Cox, *The Brady Bunch Movie* (1995)

"Be saved, you and that hip-swinging daughter of Satan!"

—Street preacher to Laurence Harvey and prostitute
Capucine, *Walk on the Wild Side* (1962)

"El Paso ain't no different from Sodom and Gomorrah."

—Frontier preacher Walter Huston,
Duel in the Sun (1946)

**"This is your *seventh* year in high school—
two as a junior, three as a senior."**

—High school principal's secretary to delinquent
Russ Tamblyn, *High School Confidential* (1958)

**"Bad manners, Mr. Boray.
The infallible sign of talent."**

—Joan Crawford, *Humoresque* (1946)

*"I shouldn'ta sit here and bother with ya, but when I like
a guy and he buys me a drink, the ceiling's the limit!"*

—Esther Howard, *Murder, My Sweet* (1944)

**"HE PROMISED ME THE WORLD—
AND I'VE GOT TO HAVE IT!"**

—Joan Crawford, *The Damned Don't Cry* (1950)

"She was a *scrubwoman*! Give her car fare, a ham at Easter, but for God's sake, don't hang around with her."

—Joni Ruth White to daughter Divine, *Polyester* (1981)

"If vee can't change de civilization here, I thought perhaps vee can go somewhere else and start vun of our own."

—Zsa Zsa Gabor to spaceship captain Eric Fleming, *Queen of Outer Space* (1958)

"I chipped my tooth on a Quaalude."

—Michelle Johnston, *Showgirls* (1995)

*"The greatest social disease of our
generation—parents!"*

—Sal Mineo, *Rock, Pretty Baby* (1959)

"I don't *like* orchids in the afternoon!"

—Joan Crawford, *Sudden Fear* (1952)

"A bedroom with only one person in it is the loneliest place in the world."

—Angela Lansbury, *Harlow* (1965)

"I'm not dead after all. The dead don't weep."

—Lana Turner, *Madame X* (1966)

Classic Camp

"Nature, Mr. Allnut, is what we're put in this world to rise above."

—Katharine Hepburn, *The African Queen* (1951)

"Fasten your seat belts. It's going to be a bumpy night."

—Bette Davis, *All About Eve* (1950)

"You have a point—an idiotic one—but a point."

—George Sanders to Marilyn Monroe, *All About Eve* (1950)

"I wouldn't worry too much about your heart. You can always put that award where your heart *ought* to be."

—Bette Davis to Anne Baxter,
All About Eve (1950)

"I'M BETSY BOOTH. I SING, YA KNOW."

—Judy Garland, *Andy Hardy Meets a Debutante* (1940)

"Are we all lit?"

—Rosalind Russell, *Auntie Mame* (1958)

"I don't go to church. Kneeling bags my nylons."

—Jan Sterling, *The Big Carnival* (1951)

"Gif me dat cobra joo-wel!"

—Maria Montez, *Cobra Woman* (1944)

"I hate dot qveen!"

—Zsa Zsa Gabor, *Queen of Outer Space* (1958)

"THE INSURANCE RAN OUT ON THE 15TH. I'D HATE TO THINK OF YOU HAVING A SMASHED FENDER OR SOMETHING WHILE YOU'RE NOT, UH, FULLY COVERED."

—Fred MacMurray to Barbara Stanwyck,
Double Indemnity (1944)

"I'M NOT GOING TO BE *IGNORED*."

—Glenn Close, *Fatal Attraction* (1987)

"Oh, Mama, all they want is my body!"

—Carroll Baker, *Harlow* (1965)

"Don't fuck with me, fellas.
This ain't my first time at the rodeo."

—Faye Dunaway, Mommie Dearest (1981)

"Oh, Jerry, don't let's ask for the moon.
We have the stars."

—Bette Davis to Paul Henreid,
Now, Voyager (1942)

"Get up, Rose, and put that tit back
in your dress!"

—Robert Duvall to Laura Dern,
Rambling Rose (1991)

"I'm an Occidental woman in an Oriental mood for love."

—Sung by Mae West, *Klondike Annie* (1936)

"I am She Who Must Be Obeyed."

—Helen Gahagan, *She* (1935)

"Why don't you come up sometime and see me?"

—Mae West, *She Done Him Wrong* (1933)

"All right, Mr. DeMille.
I'm ready for my close-up."

—Gloria Swanson, *Sunset Boulevard* (1950)

"THEN YOU MEAN, ALL THIS TIME WE COULDA BEEN FRIENDS?"

—Bette Davis to Joan Crawford, *What Ever Happened to Baby Jane?* (1962)

"Years from now, when you talk about this—and you will—be kind."

—Deborah Kerr, after sex with John Kerr, *Tea and Sympathy* (1962)

"Oh, stewardess, I speak jive."

—Barbara Billingsley,
Airplane! (1980)

"I *don't* bray!"

—Elizabeth Taylor, braying, *Who's Afraid
of Virginia Woolf?* (1966)

"I'll get you, my pretty.
And your little dog too."

—Margaret Hamilton,
The Wizard of Oz (1939)

"Toto, I have a feeling we're not in Kansas anymore!"

—Judy Garland, *The Wizard of Oz* (1939)

"Toto too!"

—Billie Burke, *The Wizard of Oz* (1939)

Select Camp Filmography

The African Queen (1951) Humphrey Bogart, Katharine Hepburn, Robert Morley. Directed by John Huston. Prim spinster meets dyspeptic boat captain in Oscar-winning classic. Not specifically a camp tour de force, but with Hepburn modeling her performance after former first lady Eleanor Roosevelt, how could it not have silly elements? Huston's innate sense of machismo kept the material from getting too flamboyant or too funny. If only someone less self-serious than James Agee had cowritten the script.

The Agony and the Ecstasy (1965) Charlton Heston, Rex Harrison, Diane Cilento. Directed by Carol Reed, best known for Oscar winners *Oliver* and *The Third Man*. Whatever one may think of the Irving Stone best-seller it was based on (and how could anyone who knows anything about Michelangelo think much of it?), the title alone symbolizes the neurotic angst that Hollywood revels in. Is there anyone in Tinsletown, from the lightest of sitcom performers to serious craftsmen, who doesn't like to think of himself as suffering, suffering, suffering for his art, who doesn't secretly compare his guest shot on, say, *Three's Company* to the painting of the Sistine Chapel? The script reflects all of Hollywood's self-interest in anguish—and includes endless breast-beating about art—but, alas, it's a bore. (It was also a giant financial disaster.)

Airplane! (1980) Peter Graves, Robert Stack, Lloyd Bridges, Leslie Nielsen, Robert Hays, Julie Hagerty. Directed by Jim Abrahams, David Zucker, and Jerry Zucker. The laughs are intentional, but no other film of the last 20 years has been so steeped in camp sensibility, from the snippiness of the "white zone—red zone" lovers' quarrel right on through to the end credits. What other film can boast Ethel Merman (in her last feature film role) as a shell-shocked flyboy who *thinks* he's Ethel Merman? Graves achieved camp immortality as the pedophiliac airline captain, but our favorite scene has passengers gleefully line up (armed with pipes, guns, and brass knuckles) to knock some sense into a hysterical passenger.

All About Eve (1950) Bette Davis, Anne Baxter, Gary Merrill, Celeste Holm, George Sanders, Hugh Marlowe, Thelma Ritter, Marilyn Monroe. Directed by Joseph Mankiewicz. For many, the mother lode. It's doubtful any film had more of an impact on gay bitchiness—in the bars, at parties—or on gay camp sensibility between 1950 and the late 1970s. Aging stage star Margo Channing (Davis) gets duped and stepped over by conniving two-facer Eve Harrington (Baxter). Sanders—dripping acid as always—breathes heavily down everyone's neck and plays yet another role (as theater critic Addison DeWitt) in which he is not—no absolutely not—gay. Cynical, sophisticated camp versus the tawdry hilarity of, say, *The Oscar*, but no less arch in its way. It's a bit too self-conscious—and for all its cynicism, a bit too self-congratulatory—for comfort. There's an awful lot of earnest swooning over the wonderfulness of "The Theater" beneath all that bitchiness. But it's a classic.

All That Heaven Allows (1955) Rock Hudson, Jane Wyman, Agnes Moorehead. Directed by Douglas Sirk (who also directed *Magnificent Obsession*, *Written on the Wind*, and *Imitation of Life*, his final film, in 1959). Eye-popping, lurid soap opera of widowed socialite Wyman falling for Thoreau-spouting, lower-class tree trimmer Hudson (with an Elvis Presley haircut), to the horror of family and friends. Even the sets reek of camp, in true Sirk style: You may want to throw away every red object in your house after seeing it. Our favorite scene: Wyman takes Hudson to a high society cocktail party to win upper-class acceptance for him. "Don't I know you from somewhere?" asks one of the pinched-faced society mavens. "You should," Hudson says, "I've been trimming your trees for three years." Her face drains of color, and the party goes downhill from there. Also memorable for a scene in which Wyman tells Hudson, "I bet you wish I were a boy." One of Rainer Werner Fassbinder's favorite films; he remade it as *Ali–Fear Eats the Soul* in 1974. He updated the tree trimmer to an Arab for relevance.

And Now Tomorrow (1944) Loretta Young, Alan Ladd, Susan Hayward, Barry Sullivan. Directed by Irving Pichel. Saintly Young plays a deaf socialite wooed by folksy doctor Ladd, who's also intent on curing her. Director Pichel also gave us the 1948 must-be-seen-to-be-believed *Miracle of the Bells* (pairing Frank Sinatra with the two-day wonder Valli), in which a beautiful movie star's grave causes a religious miracle in a small town, and the 1950 sci-fi classic *Destination Moon*, surely the only science-fiction film ever to feature a cameo by Woody Woodpecker (Woody gives viewers a crash course in aeronautical engineering).

Auntie Mame (1958) Rosalind Russell, Coral Browne, Peggy Cass, Forrest Tucker, Fred Clark. Directed by Morton DaCosta. From the novel by

Patrick Dennis. An essential part of gay cultural literacy despite the utter falseness of Dennis's heterosexuality.

The Balcony (1963) Shelley Winters, Peter Falk, Leonard Nimoy, Lee Grant. Directed by Joseph Strick. Based on the play by Jean Genet. Almost unendurable '60s schlock about sex and power, set in a brothel run by world-weary Madame Irma (Winters), who spouts so many blasé, heartless epigrams you may wonder why she isn't an editor at *The New York Review of Books*. Hard to believe this was praised by *The New Yorker* ("a shocking film worth being shocked by") and *The New York Post* ("hard-hitting cinematic art"). But then, it was the '60s, a decade that saw prominent critics falling over each other to venerate *Easy Rider* as a masterpiece. Frankly, we always thought Genet was best for masturbating over while maintaining a pretense of reading "good" literature. But then, what do we know? We've seen *Harlow* 20 times, and *Cleopatra* is one of our favorite films.

Body Heat (1981) Kathleen Turner, William Hurt, Mickey Rourke, Richard Crenna, Ted Danson. Directed by Lawrence Kasdan. Kasdan's hodgepodge of 1940s film noir clichés has Turner as a feverish femme fatale who drips ice cream on her dress and Hurt as the chump who wants to lick it off. Without the two of them it would be like reading *Bartlett's Familiar Quotations*. This was Kas-dan's directorial debut—the same year, he wrote the script for a hodgepodge of action film clichés, *Raiders of the Lost Ark*. He went on to do a hodgepodge of Western clichés in *Silverado* (1985).

The Brady Bunch Movie (1995) Shelley Long, Gary Cole, Michael McKean, with cameos by the stars of the original TV series. Directed by Betty Thomas. Go ahead, be a snob. But you risk missing one of the best (intentional) camp turns of the '90s, with Jennifer Elise Cox as long-suffering younger sister Jan slowly undergoing a psychotic break in the face of older sister Marcia's perfection. "Marcia did it again! Marcia, Marcia, Marcia!"

Butterfield 8 (1960) Elizabeth Taylor, Eddie Fisher, Laurence Harvey, Dina Merrill. Directed by Daniel Mann. Taylor as "the slut of all time," based on John O'Hara's best-seller about an expensive call girl who wants to be a nice girl after all, married to Mr. Right and giving Tupperware parties for the neighbors. "She's like a flea," one of her former clients observes. "Hop, hop, hop, from one dog to another. She bites you and she's gone." Less fun than it sounds. Taylor won the Oscar for Best Actress, though it's widely speculated to have been a sympathy vote for her various personal troubles at the time.

Camille (1937) Greta Garbo, Robert Taylor, Lionel Barrymore, Henry Daniell. Directed by George

Cukor. When Charles Ludlam did his camp send-up of *Camille* with the Ridiculous Theatrical Company in the 1970s, he managed to make audiences howl with laughter and weep at the same time; this elephantine MGM production conveys much the same effect but for different reasons. Its datedness—and the casting of handsome but uninteresting Taylor as Armand—give it a camp edge. But the heart of the film is Garbo: The camera loves her, as if she were a luminous ray of light. For anyone seeking the definitive demonstration of raw star power, this is the one to see.

Can't Stop the Music (1980) Steven Guttenberg, Valerie Perrine, Bruce Jenner, Tammy Grimes, the Village People. Directed by Nancy Walker. "You don't spend $13 million to make a minority movie!" producer Allan Carr carped when asked if his film biography of the Village People would have the seemingly inevitable gay overtones. Later, one of the disco group's members, Randy Jones ("Cowboy") told *The Advocate* he wasn't worried about losing gay fans over the film: "Look, we're making a big-budgeted movie, and movie money is conservative money—do you realize 13-year-old girls buy more of our records than anyone else?" When the film finally hit theaters, everyone—including the 13-year-old girls—stayed away. *Newsweek* critic David Ansen dubbed it, "The first all-singing, all-dancing horror film…. If this is the movie musical event of the '80s, we've got nine grim years

ahead." Double entendres abound, as do endless smirks, winks, and giggles. It's as if the cast members watched footage of slumber parties to prepare for their roles. But there is the "YMCA" number.

The Carpetbaggers (1964) George Preppard, Alan Ladd, Carroll Baker, Elizabeth Ashley, Robert Cummings, Martha Hyer. Directed by Edward Dmtryk. Preppard is Howard Hughes in this 2½ hour potboiler, adapted from Harold Robbins's best-seller. It's never as much fun as it should have been, despite Baker's big scene swinging from a crystal chandelier. Only the ever-fascinating Ashley emerges unscathed. This was Ladd's final film: He died of an overdose of sleeping pills and alcohol the year it was released.

Cleopatra (1963) Elizabeth Taylor, Richard Burton, Rex Harrison, Roddy McDowall, Martin Landau. Directed by Joseph Mankiewicz. The most publicized film of the '60s, this was the most expensive motion picture made up to that time, and the 24-month shooting schedule was punctuated by scandal and gossip, especially the off-screen romance between Taylor and Burton. The actual film is long (four hours and three minutes), often stunning to look at, and surprisingly faithful to the historical record. Still, it's wildly uneven: Gripping and literate scenes are followed by howling vacuity and grotesquely faux Shavian wit. Harrison is consistently brilliant as Julius Caesar, Burton somewhat less so as Antony. Taylor, seemingly perfect for the title role, is the film's weakest component: She's unconvincing in almost every scene and lacking in charisma. For all that, it's probably worth watching at least once, and it ranks high on many famous directors' lists of "guilty pleasures."

Cobra Woman (1944) Maria Montez, Jon Hall, Sabu. Directed by Robert Siodmak. Time hasn't been kind to the legendary camp classic—it may lull you to sleep. Fantasy tale of evil twin sisters, island love, pagan religion, and, of course, the cobra jewel. Sluggish at times, outright unendurable at others. They never should have released the actual movie, just plastered gorgeous stills of Montez everywhere. Best feature: the frenzied, nightclubbish "cobra dance." No religious ritual has ever looked more like a deranged Vegas floor show.

Crimes of Passion (1984) Kathleen Turner, John Laughlin, Anthony Perkins, Annie Potts. Directed by Ken Russell. Unjustly neglected sex drama with Turner leading a double life: She's a successful (albeit, unhappy) fashion designer by day; at night, she dons a blond wig and becomes China Blue, a Hollywood whore willing to try anything once. (The unrated European video features a scene of Turner sodomizing a police officer with his nightstick.) The screenplay—by gay screenwriter A. Scott Berg—crackles with real wit, and Russell's direction is, for him, remarkably restrained.

The Egyptian (1954) Edmund Purdom, Jean Simmons, Victor Mature, Gene Tierney, Peter Ustinov, Michael Wilding, Henry Daniell, John Carradine, Bella Darvi. Directed by Michael Curtiz. One of Hollywood's they-died-for-their-beautiful-religious-beliefs spectacles. Less engrossing (and less prestigious) than *The Robe* but far funnier. Purdom is the court physician caught up in nasty doings in ancient Thebes. He ruins himself over lust for glittering temptress Darvi (in assorted colored tinsel wigs) but redeems himself at the end by embracing one God. The amazing thing is Tierney. As pharaoh's conniving sister she inexplicably affects a low, growling voice and the padded-shoulder mannerisms of a linebacker: She seems to think she's in *The Killing of Sister Hatshepsut.*

Fatal Attraction (1987) Glenn Close, Michael Douglas, Anne Archer. Directed by Adrian Lyne. The *Reefer Madness* of infidelity. Imbecilic tale of married man Douglas who has a one-night stand with Close; she turns psychotic and begins stalking him and his family. Perfect entertainment for the AIDS-panicked middle classes of the mid 1980s. Just plain camp to anyone else with half a brain. Boiled bunnies, anyone?

The Female Animal (1958) Hedy Lamarr, George Nader, Jane Powell, Jan Sterling. Directed by Harry Keller. By 1958 Lamarr's screen career was almost nonexistent, and she was desperate for work. *The*

Female Animal is an act of desperation for all concerned. It's fun to watch (especially wisecracking Sterling), but you're aware of an uncomfortable edge running through your reaction to it, as if you'd suddenly run into the real Norma Desmond at a Goodwill store. It's all about show business, happiness, business, booze, sex—the usual crap. Camp lines abound. Nearly any film in which poor Nader is the leading man is guaranteed to be full of them.

Flame of Araby (1951) Jeff Chandler, Maureen O'Hara. Directed by Charles Lamont (best known for many of the Ma and Pa Kettle and Abbott and Costello features). Chandler woos O'Hara on the deserts of the Universal backlot, but, truth be told, he's a lot more interested in horses. Another colorful example of the men-must-act-like-snitty-12-year-olds-so-women-can-connive-even-harder-to-snare-them school of filmmaking. Chandler's name in the credits is almost as certain a guarantee of camp hilarity as George Nader's. (The exception is his Oscar-nominated performance in *Broken Arrow*.) Coproduced by Ross Hunter.

Harlow (1965) Carroll Baker, Red Buttons, Angela Lansbury, Peter Lawford, Mike Connors, Leslie Nielsen, Martin Balsom, Raf Vallone. Directed by Gordon Douglas. Produced by Joseph E. Levine. In the mid 1960s there were two film biographies of Jean Harlow being rushed into production. The other (and first to be released)

starred Carol Lynley and is all but forgotten. The Baker version was the slicker and more expensive of the two. Producer Levine reputedly drove everyone involved so hard that Baker was taken to the hospital from exhaustion when shooting was finished. Everything about it is wrong—especially the facts. So why is it so damned watchable and oddly poignant? Almost every frame of it looks hand-tinted with lipstick and nail polish.

Love Has Many Faces (1965) Lana Turner, Cliff Robertson, Hugh O'Brian, Stefanie Powers, Ruth Roman. Directed by Alexander Singer. Overheated tale of male prostitutes and lonely middle-aged women on the beaches of Acapulco, Mexico. It's the kind of film where women get kisses they're disgusted by and smear them off with the back of their hand—but they always come back for more. "You'll do anything for money," gigolo Ron Husman tells fellow hustler O'Brian with contempt. "That's the thing about money, buddy," O'Brian replies, lying facedown in bed in his boxer shorts, "It wrinkles, but it never grows old." Apparently, love has only one face, and it looks an awful lot like the portrait on a $100 bill.

Madame X (1966) Lana Turner, John Forsythe, Ricardo Montalban, Burgess Meredith, Constance Bennett, Keir Dullea. Directed by David Lowell Rich. Produced by Ross Hunter. Hunter—who gained notoriety producing such weepy classics as *Magnificent Obsession*, *Imitation of Life*, *Midnight Lace*, and the 1973 megabomb musical *Lost Horizon*—gives us the "riches to rags" saga of tragic Turner, forced to abandon her marriage and her son because of scandal. Twenty years later (after becoming a dissolute woman), she goes on trial for murdering a man and is defended by her now-all-grown-up son (Dullea), who doesn't know that she's his mother. The story—filmed at least six other times, including in 1981, with Tuesday Weld in the title role—ends with Turner peacefully dying on a jail cell cot before the judge can send her to the gas chamber.

Mildred Pierce (1945) Joan Crawford, Ann Blyth, Eve Arden, Zachary Scott, Jack Carson. Directed by Michael Curtiz. Crawford thought that winning an Oscar for this film meant a whole new glamorous beginning to her career. Oops. Ten years later (and by then well into her 50s), she was playing understandably nervous femme fatales in cheap films like *Female on the Beach*. Blyth—who later garnered a new generation of fans by hawking Hostess cupcakes on TV—plays Crawford's spoiled, insatiable daughter. Crawford, blind to how she's being used, will do anything, anything for her. Naturally, it ends in tragedy: step-incest and murder. The entire thing is better than it should be; you can thank director Curtiz for that. Still, Carol Burnett had it right when she named her parody of this classic Warner Bros. melodrama *Mildred Fierce*.

Miss Sadie Thompson (1953) Rita Hayworth, Aldo Ray, Jose Ferrer, Charles Bronson. Directed by Curtis Bernhardt. Entertaining, watered-down version of W. Somerset Maugham story "Rain," with Hayworth as a hooker stranded on a Pacific island with 7,000 horny marines and a Bible-thumping missionary determined to bring her to her knees, in more ways than one. Hayworth is unexpectedly subdued—she's dropped the fierce sensuality of *Gilda* and tromps through much of the film like a disgruntled football coach. But Ray—was there ever an actor who better embodied the saying, "If you can't eat it or fuck it, then piss on it"? In this version Sadie runs off to married, middle-class happiness with Ray in Australia! Several songs, including "I'm Getting the Blue Pacific Blues."

Now, Voyager (1942) Bette Davis, Paul Henreid, Claude Rains, Gladys Cooper. Directed by Irving Rapper. Davis delivers knockout performance as ugly duckling spinster (in the early scenes she looks like Leonid Brezhnev) transformed into a stunning, happy woman through the care of psychiatrist Rains. The moment when we first glimpse her complete metamorphosis—she steps onto the gangplank of a tourist boat—is one of the high points of 1940s cinema. The not-so-believable love story between her and Henreid is actually secondary to the film. What most people relate to is the exhilaration (and precariousness of Davis's suddenly discovered freedom. It's a great film.

129

The Prodigal (1955) Lana Turner, Edmund Purdom, Louis Calhern, Neville Brand, Walter Hampden, Henry Daniell, Joseph Wiseman. Directed by Richard Thorpe. Jesus Christ was smarter than MGM executives: He kept the story down to a parable. Endless, glossy, amazingly unsexy saga of devout Purdom lured to his doom by fascination for pagan high priestess Turner. Interesting as one of the only films in which Daniell was cast in a sympathetic role—you're so used to seeing him greedy and vicious, it gives a jolt to see him returning a starving old woman's money to her.

Suddenly, Last Summer (1959) Elizabeth Taylor, Katherine Hepburn, Montgomery Clift, Mercedes McCambridge, Albert Dekker. Directed by Joseph Mankiewicz. It's like *The Towering Inferno* or *The Poseidon Adventure*: You wait for each new eye-popping atrocity and then lick your lips thinking, *There's a juicy one*. Cannibalism, lobotomies, carnivorous plants, cruel nuns, sex-starved asylum inmates—you know you're firmly in camp country when, in the opening scene, Clift is performing a delicate lobotomy while plaster falls from the walls and the lights are flickering on and off. That people take this twaddle seriously is hard to believe. (Leonard Maltin gives it 3½ stars, and deems it "fascinating.") For us it will always be one of a handful of films at camp ground zero, as funny as anything Carol Burnett ever came up with. Just try to keep a straight face when Taylor,

ravishing in form-fitting convent hand-me-downs, tells Clift, "You may not believe it, but I can be quite nice to look at when I'm all cleaned up."

The Ten Commandments (1956) Charlton Heston, Yul Brynner, Anne Baxter, Edward G. Robinson, Debra Paget, Vincent Price, Cedric Hardwicke, Yvonne De Carlo, John Derek. Directed by Cecil B. DeMille. Biblical excess leads to high camp in DeMille's nearly four-hour saga of Moses leading the Hebrews out of Egypt. Sidesplitting, misguided dialogue vies with occasionally scenery-chewing performances for the viewer's credulity—and amusement. (DeMille filmed the story once before, in 1923, but it wasn't nearly as ripe.) Baxter—as sex-starved Princess Nefertari, tirelessly conniving to bed high-minded Heston—has all the best lines:

"What is there in the mud of those slave pits that could keep you out of my arms?"

"You call yourself a prophet, a man of God, but I know better."

"Oh, Moses, Moses, why of all men did I fall in love with the prince of fools?"

And who can forget the priceless shot of Brynner and Baxter—the pharaoh and his queen—limp and depressed on their respective thrones (while the Hebrews are hundreds of miles away having a heyday), looking for all the world not like monarchs but two suburban chumps who have just smashed up the family BMW? While some of De-Mille's early films—*The Sign of the Cross* (1932) and *The Crusades* (1935), for example—have their camp moments, they actually reveal a strikingly original director's vision, full of luminous and memorable images, before he became obsessed with oversized schlock in the 1940s.

Torch Song (1953) Joan Crawford, Michael Wilding, Gig Young, Harry Morgan, Marjorie Rambeau, Nancy Gates. Directed by Charles Walters. Crawford is an all-devouring Broadway actress who falls in love with a blind concert pianist (Wilding); he tries to soften her bitterness and show her the real meaning of life. The only film—count your blessings—to feature Crawford in blackface (for one of her big musical numbers). Our favorite scene: Crawford chats with her mother about the seemingly impossible romance with Wilding. "But he's blind!" Crawford finally bellows in exasperation. "Oh, well," her mother blithely replies. "Your father was a little bald when I met him."

The Unguarded Moment (1956) Esther Williams, George Nader, Edward Andrews, John Saxon, Jack Albertson. Directed by Harry Keller. From a story by Rosalind Russell. In a rare nonhydraulic role, Williams plays an earnest high school teacher who can't understand why her tight sweaters are stirring up impure impulses in her male students. Her after-school tutoring doesn't help. "Sandy," she tells one boy, "you have a touch of the tiger in you." Saxon, barely 20 at the time, makes up for the dull stretches: He fills out his jeans as emphatically as Williams fills a brassiere.

Valley of the Dolls (1967) Barbara Parkins, Patty Duke, Sharon Tate, Susan Hayward. Directed by Mark Robson. Juicy trashola fashioned by Twentieth Century Fox from one of Jacqueline Susann's ribs: It's 123 minutes of undiluted camp heaven. Too many wallow-worthy scenes to recount, but standouts include Duke flushing Hayward's wig down the toilet and Tony Scotti as an achingly handsome nightclub singer stricken by a disease that leaves him a mental incompetent; his big scene comes when he croons a love song in the lunatic asylum. The other inmates are breathless. Classic film score was one of the first for John Williams (billed here as "Johnny"), who went on to fame with *Jaws*, *Star Wars*, *E.T.*, and others.

Walk on the Wild Side (1962) Capucine, Laurence Harvey, Barbara Stanwyck, Jane Fonda, Anne Baxter. Directed by Edward Dmytryk (*The Carpetbaggers*). Dreary doings in New Orleans bordello with lesbian Stanwyck in charge and ravishing Capucine, her favorite piece of merchandise. Harvey staggers through his role (as he did every other) with the pallid tightness of a man in the throes of angina—he's seen here trying to woo Capucine back to suburban happiness. Has anyone ever made a film set in a whorehouse that wasn't fatuous, silly, and drab? Come to think of it, they have—Lizzie Borden's consistently pleasurable *Working Girls* (1986).

Week-End in Havana (1941) Carmen Miranda, Alice Faye, John Payne, Cesar Romero. Directed by Walter Lang. Who can ever remember what these films are about after seeing them—or, at the very least, who can keep one of Miranda's film straight from another? Her films are the camp equivalent of raspberry cheesecake. A steady diet would make you queasy—but is life really worth living without them?

What Ever Happened to Baby Jane? (1962) Bette Davis, Joan Crawford, Anna Lee, Victor Buono. Directed by Robert Aldrich. Anyone who's spent more than a passing moment on Hollywood Boulevard knows the accuracy of Aldrich's rich masterpiece about two show business sisters—one a popular child performer, the other a successful movie actress—and their battle of wills in a funereal stucco home in Los Angeles. The house itself, done up like a piss-elegant mortuary, is a metaphor for Hollywood: No ray of sunlight is ever admitted, and the real world can only be glimpsed through barred windows. At the time of the film's release, critics tended to regard the film as "a hoot," a kind of gothic in-joke; the darker complexity of the story has only increased in reputation through the years. Crawford has the easier, gentler role: wheelchair-bound, seemingly noble, long-suffering. (Though it's hard to watch her without thinking of Christina and the Bon Ami can.) But it's Davis who delivers the tour de force. Who can forget the scene in which she stares into the mirror, with devastating overhead lighting, and suddenly confronts the deranged clown mask that has become her face? It's a cautionary tale not only for faded celebrities but for an awful lot of gay men as well. Needlessly remade as a TV movie in 1991 with the Redgrave sisters in the leads.

The Women (1939) Norma Shearer, Rosalind Russell, Joan Crawford, Paulette Goddard, Joan Fontaine, Mary Boland, Ruth Hussey, Marjorie Main. Directed by George Cukor. Adapted from the play by Clare Booth Luce. Like the inevitably disappointing first glimpse of Radio City Music Hall, this legendary bitchfest seems surprisingly small on first viewing. Its reputation is far more energetic than the reality. The cattiness seems more than a little moldy now. But then it's from the pen of Luce—no Dorothy Parker, she. See it for the same reason you would travel out of your way to glimpse the Liberty Bell: as a part of broadening your understanding of cracked but important things.

132

Index of Films Cited